The Geological Column

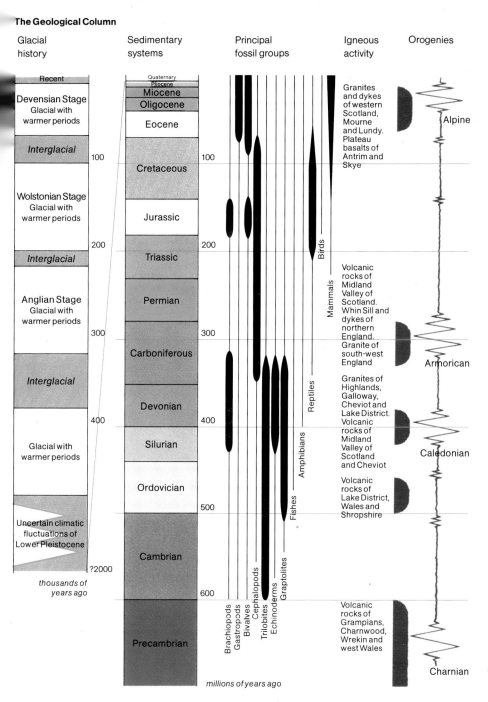

the soil, but with some extra consideration it will yield a three-dimensional view of the structure of the uppermost crust of the earth, of the relationship of one rock formation to another, of the probable nature of the subsurface solid geology below its concealing mantle of unconsolidated sediment or drift. And even beyond these facts of space, the map enables one to look back in time to the land as it has evolved throughout the ages, from the very formation of the rocks themselves through the succession of environments which has moulded them in their present shapes, to the countryside of today, attractive or dull, rich or barren.

Contents

1

Creation of the rocks

Sediments

First of all consider the rocks themselves. The primeval rocks were igneous, solidifying from a melt at a time when vast amounts of gas and water vapour were escaping from the cooling crust. The atmosphere so created brought about the beginnings of erosion of these rocks, yielding the very first sediments. Everyone is familiar with the accumulation of sediment. Muds, silts and sands settle in ditches, ponds and streams. If you shake up such a mixture in a jar of water the particles will settle slowly, the heaviest at the bottom, in layers or strata. Similar processes operate on a large scale in rivers, estuaries, deltas and oceans.

Whatever the materials, they are almost invariably laid down as nearly horizontal layers, although locally still subject to disturbance. Thus a sudden influx of flood-water, or a minor earth tremor, may mobilise the soft sediments on an inclined sea floor and cause them to flow downslope as a turbidity current or semi-liquid sludge.

Sediments also form on land. Wind-blown sands become dune-bedded sandstones, and screes may form breccias. Glaciers and meltwater streams deposit boulder clays and gravels, and these and other drift deposits, such as the alluvial silts of rivers and estuaries and the weathered debris of head, totally obscure large areas of the solid geology underneath.

Dead organisms provide fossils which permit the correlation of strata of similar age at widely separated localities, and this simple concept has dictated the division of the geological column of the last 600 million years.

1 Sedimentation

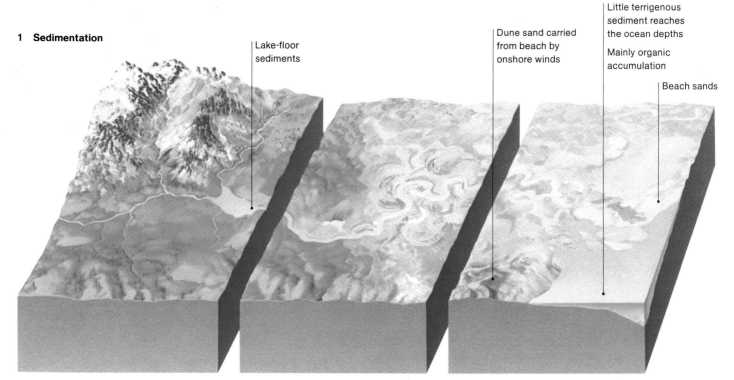

Lake-floor sediments

Dune sand carried from beach by onshore winds

Little terrigenous sediment reaches the ocean depths

Mainly organic accumulation

Beach sands

Erosion by fast-flowing highland streams
Accumulation of scree

Deposition of alluvium on flood plain of slow meandering river

Submarine deposition of river-borne sediments; coarse inshore, finer offshore

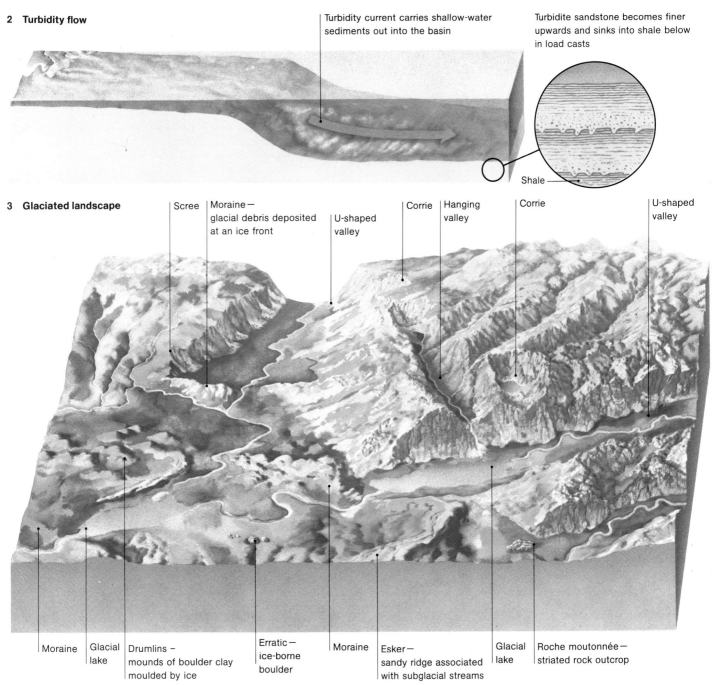

2 Turbidity flow

Turbidity current carries shallow-water sediments out into the basin

Turbidite sandstone becomes finer upwards and sinks into shale below in load casts

Shale

3 Glaciated landscape

Scree

Moraine — glacial debris deposited at an ice front

U-shaped valley

Corrie

Hanging valley

Corrie

U-shaped valley

Moraine

Glacial lake

Drumlins – mounds of boulder clay moulded by ice

Erratic — ice-borne boulder

Moraine

Esker — sandy ridge associated with subglacial streams

Glacial lake

Roche moutonnée — striated rock outcrop

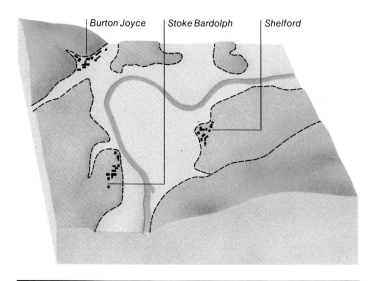

4 River terraces

The River Trent near Nottingham once flowed at a higher level and has since cut down to form the present alluvial plain, leaving the older (higher) alluvium as a river terrace. Villages within the valley have tended to grow more on the better drained terrace soils than on the modern alluvium.

Extracted from geological map sheet 126: Nottingham
BRG The Pennines and adjacent areas (8) and BRG Central England (10)

5 Unconformity

A break in the depositional sequence representing a period of time with no surviving sedimentary record.

North-west of Bath, Keuper Marl rests unconformably on older strata and is in turn overlain unconformably by the Rhaetic.

Extracted from geological sheet 265: Bath
BRG Bristol and Gloucester District (16)

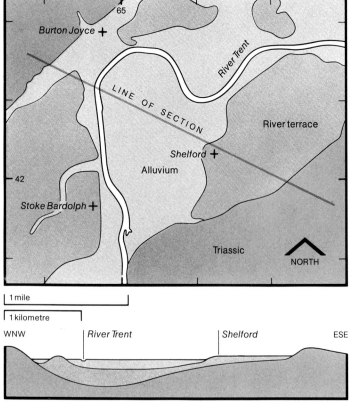

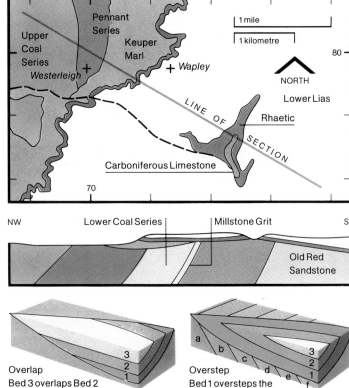

Overlap
Bed 3 overlaps Bed 2
which overlaps Bed 1

Overstep
Bed 1 oversteps the
progressively older beds f to a

6 Igneous activity

Molten rock rising through the crust of the earth solidifies in a variety of forms and may break surface through volcanic vents.

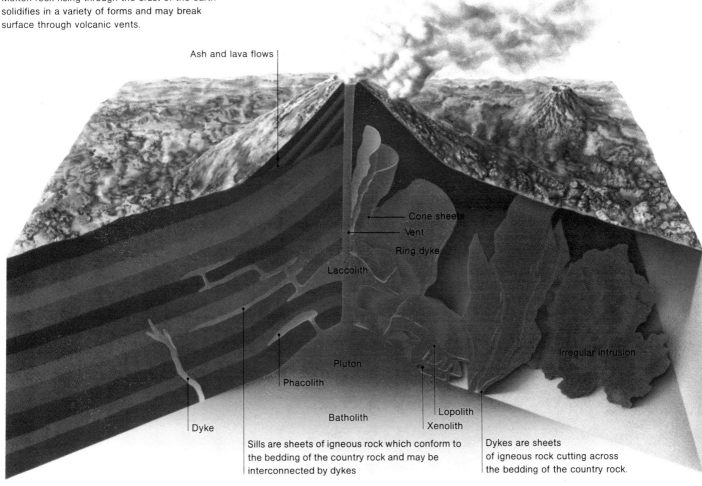

Ash and lava flows

Cone sheets

Vent

Ring dyke

Laccolith

Pluton

Phacolith

Dyke

Batholith

Lopolith

Xenolith

Irregular intrusion

Sills are sheets of igneous rock which conform to the bedding of the country rock and may be interconnected by dykes

Dykes are sheets of igneous rock cutting across the bedding of the country rock.

Magmas and metamorphism

Stresses within the earth may facilitate the emplacement of igneous rocks. Release of pressure permits superheated rock deep in the crust to liquefy and rise as a magma – through fractures, by shouldering aside overlying rocks or by engulfing, mobilising and assimilating them. Huge masses of magma whose progress is arrested at depth cool slowly to develop a coarsely crystalline texture. Smaller quantities penetrating narrow fissures cool more quickly and are finer grained, while the lavas which pour out from volcanoes may, when solidified, be so fine as to appear glassy.

Intrusion of a magma can induce changes in adjacent rocks as their mineral grains crystallise or react in response to heat and pressure. Compression by earth movement causes flaky minerals such as mica to grow in sediments at right angles to the direction of stress, locally destroying all traces of any original bedding. And these two causes of metamorphism, heat and pressure, affect pre-existing rocks, both sedimentary and igneous, in varying degrees up to and including melting.

7 Folds

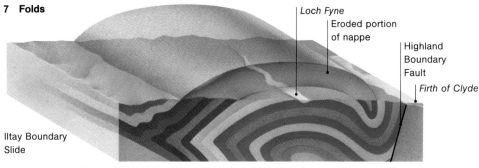

Loch Fyne
Eroded portion of nappe
Highland Boundary Fault
Firth of Clyde
Iltay Boundary Slide

The Tay Nappe of the southern Grampians extends parallel to its axis south-westwards right across Scotland and into Ireland

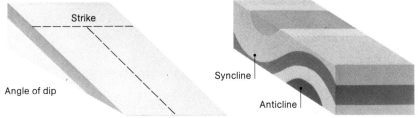

Strike

Angle of dip

The dip of a bed is measured from the horizontal and is perpendicular to the direction of strike

Syncline
Anticline

Simple folding produces arches (anticlines) and basins (synclines)

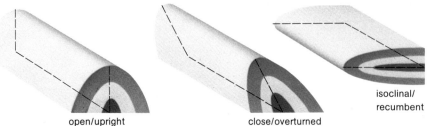

isoclinal/recumbent

open/upright

close/overturned

Fold style: A decrease in the angle between the limbs of a fold represents an increase in 'tightness' and is illustrated by the sequence open–close–isoclinal

The inclination of the axial plane of a fold is described by the sequence upright–overturned–recumbent

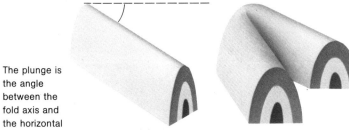

The plunge is the angle between the fold axis and the horizontal

Refolded fold: The only evidence of such structures may be two intersecting cleavages, parallel to the axial planes of the early and later folds

6 CREATION OF THE ROCKS   Folding and faulting

8 Faults

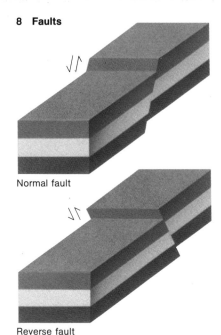

Normal fault

Reverse fault

The vertical displacement or downthrow on a normal or reverse fault may be a few inches or some thousands of feet

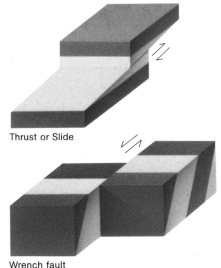

Thrust or Slide

Wrench fault

Displacements along thrusts or wrench faults range up to many miles

Folding and faulting

Earth movements, now largely attributed to the slow impact of great crustal plates, have produced tilting, flexuring, folding, fracturing and translocation of strata. Several orogenies, or peaks of such activity, are known to have occurred. During the most recent, which produced the Alps and the Himalayas around 20 to 40 million years ago, Britain lay on the fringe of the movements, but at earlier times our rocks have been subjected to immense stresses. Thus the nappes of the Alps, huge flat-lying overfolds which have been pushed horizontally for long distances, resemble similar but older structures in the Grampians.

Fracturing of the upper crust may be a response to the same pressure which caused folding, driving one block up and over another either at a steep angle to create a reversed fault or at a gentle angle to create a thrust or slide. Relaxation of pressure permits the settling of blocks under the influence of gravity, with the formation of normal faults. Wrench faults are those in which the relative movement is horizontal, but in many faults both vertical and horizontal components are present.

Minor movements

Finally, when the major forces are spent and a stable block of country is undergoing normal erosion – and this is the situation in Britain today – smaller displacements of a strictly local nature may yet affect the surface strata. Hard beds capping watersheds sag into the valleys, both by squeezing out underlying clays and by actually slipping downhill. These cambers are widespread in the Jurassic rocks of the Midlands and the Cretaceous strata of the south-east.

Stretching of the hard bed leads to fissures or gulls trending parallel to the contours, and the squeezed clays are commonly twisted and contorted in the lower ground as valley bulges.

Other gravity-induced structures include mud flows and landslips, both of which generally depend on lubrication by water. The largest slips in Britain are probably those affecting Jurassic sediments and Tertiary lavas along the north-east coast of Skye.

9 Minor movements

Cambers, gulls and valley bulging.

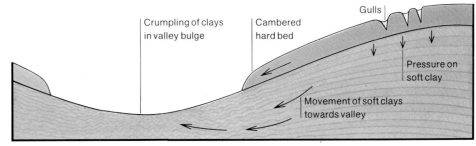

- Crumpling of clays in valley bulge
- Cambered hard bed
- Gulls
- Pressure on soft clay
- Movement of soft clays towards valley

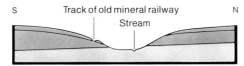

S — Track of old mineral railway — Stream — N

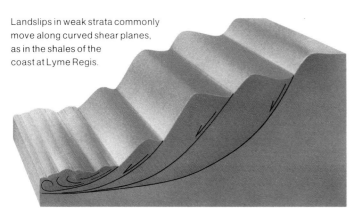

Landslips in weak strata commonly move along curved shear planes, as in the shales of the coast at Lyme Regis.

At Horley, near Banbury, cambers of Marlstone Rock Bed, a ferruginous limestone, locally almost obscure the underlying Middle Lias silts.

Extracted from geological map sheet 201: Banbury
BRG Central England (10)
BRG London and the Thames Valley (13)
BRG South-West England (17)

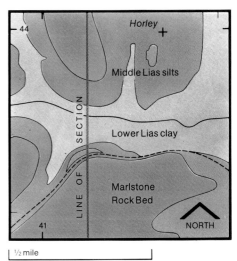

- Horley
- Middle Lias silts
- Lower Lias clay
- Marlstone Rock Bed
- LINE OF SECTION
- NORTH
- 44
- 41
- ½ mile
- 1 kilometre

Making the map

These, then, are some of the problems that may have confronted the geological surveyor who made your map. His direct observations are supplemented by old mining information, a variety of sophisticated techniques for instrumental survey, and aerial photography.

The geologist enters a new area, using as his field sheet an Ordnance Survey map at a scale of six inches to a mile, or perhaps 1:10 000. The foundations of his map are the outcrops of bare rock. On the coast there may be extensive cliffs, in which the geology is depicted in full detail but whose examination requires a great deal of time. Inland each river, stream and ditch is followed, and sporadic exposures plotted. Quarries are a fruitful source of data, as are wells and boreholes and cuttings for road or railway. Temporary sections may be available in foundation trenches, and even where excavations have been filled there is usually enough debris scattered at surface to indicate rock types. Shallow cross-country sections are afforded by trenches dug for main services. Mineralised areas generally contain old shafts and adits; the former are commonly accompanied by spoil heaps and the latter accessible for at least a few yards. Active mining fields furnish underground data which permit increased understanding of the three-dimensional geological structure.

The surveyor records his data on map or in notebook. He identifies the rocks, sampling if necessary, and measures the section. Textural and mineralogical characteristics are noted. In the case of sediments the inclination (dip) and trend (strike) are measured and cleavage nature and attitude determined. If folds are present the dips of both limbs are recorded, together with the trends and plunges (inclination) of the fold axes. Even where fold hinges are not visible, evidence of younging – the direction in which younger beds come on – in adjacent exposures may indicate the pattern of folding. And without even this, a large number of dip measurements when plotted as a statistical study may reveal the attitudes of the main fold limbs.

The surveyor notes the nature of any lineation on the rock surfaces, checks for signs of inversion, searches for and collects fossils and observes any faults or fractures in the section. These may be so small that correlation between the beds on one side and those on the other is obvious. But even when the relationship is not wholly clear, the attitude of strata adjoining the fault may show the sense of movement. The fracture itself may be characterised by shattering of rock and may have afforded a channel for mineralised fluids.

Igneous rocks possess textures which reflect the crystallisation process and may exhibit flow structures. Where their contacts with country rock are visible, evidence of discordance (cutting across bedding) or concordance (alignment with bedding) may be available. Nature of rock and margin distinguish between intrusion (injection into country rock) and extrusion (eruption at surface). If the igneous mass is in the form of a sheet its inclination must be measured or calculated, just as in the case of a sedimentary bed. Similarly, the orientations of all joints, fractures showing no displacement, are recorded. Two igneous bodies in contact one with the other will show which is the younger and afford a valuable clue to the sequence of intrusion.

Had the surveyor plotted only these direct observations, his field sheet would probably still be mainly blank, with local concentrations of data along certain stream courses or in quarries. Between these areas of good exposure, lines are drawn by interpretation, inference and use of a hand auger. Surface brash (rock debris) is a good guide only when it is plentiful.

Most important of all in interpretation is land form. Differences in rock type generally mean differing resistance to erosion, and hence find expression in topography. The surveyor maps all such 'features', even though the significance of some may not be apparent then or ever. It is possible to trace geological boundaries across country by following a slight change of slope. Faults may be found to be aligned with valleys or with 'dog-leg' disruptions of stream courses. Displacement of features whose nature remains a mystery is nevertheless a guide to lines of fracture.

Natural vegetation is of assistance but reflects soils, not rocks, and distinctions are blurred by soil creep, leaching and the downhill movement of minerals in groundwater. Local buildings and walls afford similar help in upland 'stone country' such as Exmoor, the Cotswolds and the Pennines.

Drift deposits must be mapped and correlated in the same detail as the solid geology—upon which they rest as a mantle but to whose structure they bear little or no relation. Boulders deposited by ancient glaciers may be identified with distant outcrops, so pointing towards the source of the ice, and parallel scratches cut in solid rock indicate local directions of ice movement.

10 Geology and topography

Geological boundaries and contours almost coincide at Edge Hill, Warwickshire, a prominence from which the royalist army fought the battle of 23 October 1642. The minor sinuosites of the Marlstone Rock Bed outcrop are due to cambering.

Wenlock Edge in Shropshire is both a piece of Housman nostalgia and a scarp of Silurian limestone.

Extracted from geological map sheets 166 and 201: Church Stretton and Banbury.
BRG The Welsh Borderland (11) and BRG Central England (10)

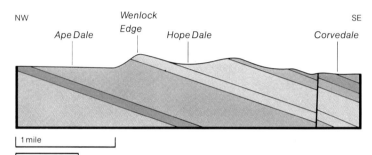

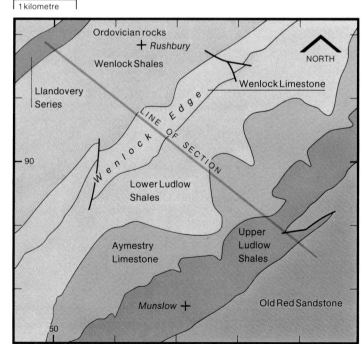

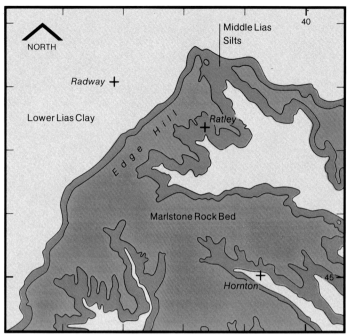

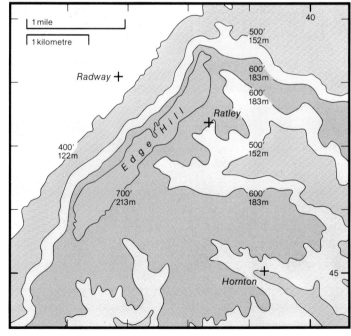

Perhaps the most difficult country of all for the geologist is the urban area. A few outcrops remain, and natural features are still discernible in places, but much is obscured. A great deal of the mapping depends upon temporary excavations at the time of survey, and such records of older similar diggings, wells and boreholes which have been preserved by local authorities and commercial companies.

It has been possible to indicate only some of the more important techniques of geological survey, and the symbols illustrated are likewise a selection. Fact, deduction, an eye for country and the ability to think in three dimensions are all vital to the making of a geological map.

Let us follow our surveyor into one or two areas of Britain of contrasting geology, and look at a few of the difficulties that face him and some of the conclusions he draws.

The mountainous part of Skye is a region of igneous rocks which have resisted erosion. Apart from the high peaks of the Cuillins there are no major problems of access. However, fixing a position is not easy in an area which, although small, retains the character of primitive wildness. Reference points are few, and the higher ground is frequently enveloped in cloud or mist.

It is a centre of Tertiary volcanicity, an age of igneous activity perhaps unparalleled in the history of Britain. Examination of rock types and their interrelationships reveals that the oldest igneous rocks are basaltic lavas lying partly around, but mainly north of, the hills, and piled up flow upon flow to a thickness of about 2000 feet. Close examination of the rocks reveals that beds of ash or pyroclastic fragments are rare, indicating but few explosive eruptions in a period of upwelling of basalt through vents and fissures. That the activity was intermittent is attested by the development of soils between the flows. Exposures are plentiful and the limits of the lavas readily traced. They have yielded a fairly rich brown soil on which is concentrated most of the crofting.

Evidence of the invasion and baking of one rock by another shows that the ultrabasic rock peridotite represents the earliest of the plutonic masses in Skye. These rocks were pushed up as magmas, which cooled beneath a great thickness of lava without breaking surface. Thin veins of gabbro cutting peridotite, and the presence of scattered fragments of peridotite in the gabbro, prove to the surveyor that the latter is the younger rock. It is the gabbro which now forms the Cuillin Hills. The adjacent Red Hills are made of granite, which is found to have intruded the gabbro and is therefore younger still.

Extracted from geological map sheets 166 and 201: Church Stretton and Banbury.

11 Drift

Drifts, such as peat (brown), glacial deposits (blue), and river sediments (yellow), form a superficial mantle unrelated to the geological structure beneath.

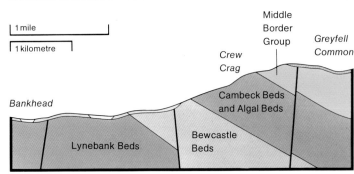

The final phase of activity is represented by predominantly basic dykes and sheets, which are found to cut across all the earlier igneous rocks. They contribute to a marked contrast in the appearance of the hills. The Red Hills have weathered uniformly to semi-rounded outlines, but in the Cuillins the dykes have clearly proved less resistant to weathering than has the gabbro. Gashes and gullies have been cut through these uplands, leaving a jagged skyline of ridges and pinnacles.

Thus the surveyor working in this part of central Skye, an area of well-exposed plutonic and volcanic rocks, needs to be able to identify the igneous rock types and deduce from their relationships the sequence of emplacement. Beyond that, his observations tell him a story of glacier movement within the hills, of how Loch Coruisk occupies a basin gouged out by ice to well below present sea level, and of how its waters intersect a moraine of glacial drift as they escape south to the sea.

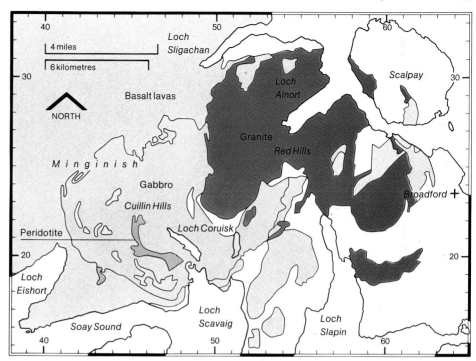

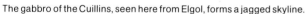

The gabbro of the Cuillins, seen here from Elgol, forms a jagged skyline.

The rounded outline of the Red Hills granite (seen above Broadford) contrasts with that of the Cuillins.

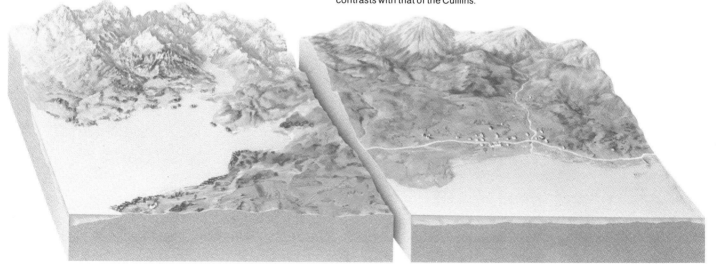

13 Wenlock Edge

Scarp and Dale country

Contrast the drifts as they appear on map and section, and compare the solid geology on Figure 10.

Extracted from 1:25 000 geological map sheet SO 59: Wenlock Edge
BRG The Welsh Borderland (11)

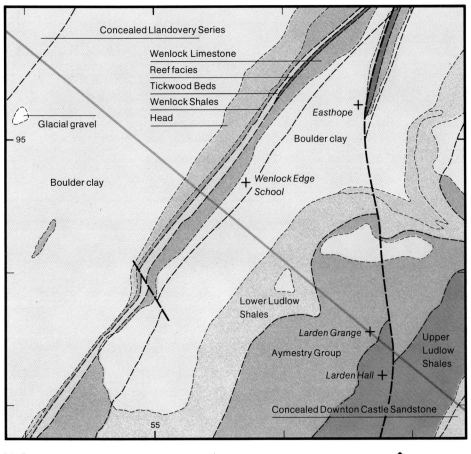

Concealed Llandovery Series

Wenlock Limestone

Reef facies

Tickwood Beds

Wenlock Shales

Head

Glacial gravel

Easthope

Boulder clay

95

Boulder clay

Wenlock Edge School

Lower Ludlow Shales

Larden Grange

Aymestry Group

Upper Ludlow Shales

Larden Hall

Concealed Downton Castle Sandstone

55

1 mile

1 kilometre

NORTH

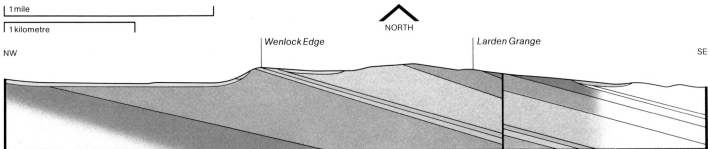

NW

Wenlock Edge

Larden Grange

SE

The hill country around Wenlock Edge in southern Shropshire is in sharp contrast. It is a landscape of scarps and dales, the product of alternating fossiliferous hard and soft beds of Silurian age which dip around 10 degrees to the south-east. Approaching from the west our surveyor traverses the Wenlock Shales of Ape Dale, the earthy limestones and limy siltstones of the Tickwood Beds on the scarp slope of Wenlock Edge, the overlying Wenlock Limestone, the Lower Ludlow Shales of Hope Dale, the Aymestry limestones of the succeeding crest, and the Upper Ludlow Shales of Corve Dale. Conformably upon this last formation rests the famous Ludlow Bone Bed, about two inches of sandy mudstone packed with fish remains and other debris, above which is the Downton Castle Sandstone.

Erratics, rock fragments foreign to the area, collected from the boulder clay mapped in Ape Dale and Hope Dale include some which match rocks of the Lake District, whence the ice may be presumed to have travelled. A single small patch of glacial sand and gravel rests on the boulder clay. Clays which have crept down-slope towards the end of, and after, the Ice Age have accumulated in mappable thicknesses along the foot of Wenlock Edge and at Moor Hall; they contain stones of the locality and are mapped as head.

Thus at Wenlock Edge our surveyor is assisted by a correlation of geological formations with topography and by the absence of major dislocations. But he must build up a knowledge of the fossil content of the rocks, he must decide where to draw his lines when the passage of one formation into another is gradational, he must bear in mind in areas of limited exposure and mixed rock assemblages that sporadic outcrops may not be typical of their parent formation. And over considerable tracts his interpretations are bedevilled by thin drifts.

We have stepped briefly into two classic areas of British geology. Perhaps it is time to take some of the gilt off the gingerbread. Bratton Clovelly, in western Devon and typical of the Culm Measures countryside, is underlain by shales with interbedded siltstones and fine-grained sandstones. In general these arenaceous beds are less than a foot thick and subordinate to the shales, but locally they form mappable units of thicker-bedded sandstones with thin shales. Fossils are rare.

Some of these sandstone units give rise to ridges, but not all such sandstones form ridges and not all ridges are sandstone. Quite commonly the topography defies explanation—it may be due to faulting, folding, ancient river systems unrelated to the present drainage or a combination of factors. Speculation and uncertainty have taken over from fact and deduction, and feature-mapping is no reliable guide to the geology.

Measured dips show that the strata have been crumpled into folds overturned to the south or south-south-east. Dislocation of sandstone units points to the presence of faults running from north-west to south-east, but the evidence of intensity of earth movement makes it certain that much more faulting exists than can be traced. The surveyor has made a map, but he is unable to interpret it except in general terms. There is no means of correlating mapped lithological groups. In his quest for a detailed understanding of the three dimensional geology, our surveyor has failed.

14 Bratton Clovelly

Insufficient evidence is available to determine the major structures.

A few only of the possibilities along the line of section are suggested diagrammatically.

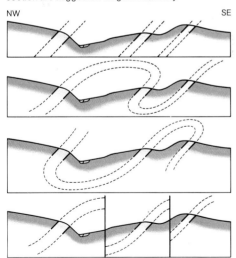

Extracted from geological map sheet 323: Holsworthy
BRG South-West England (17)

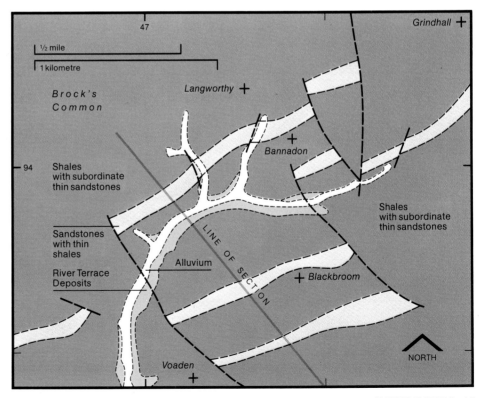

15 Burton Dassett

Typical Jurassic country in which geology is
perfectly reflected in topography

Extracted from geological map sheet 201: Banbury
BRG Central England (10) and BRG London and the Thames Valley (13)

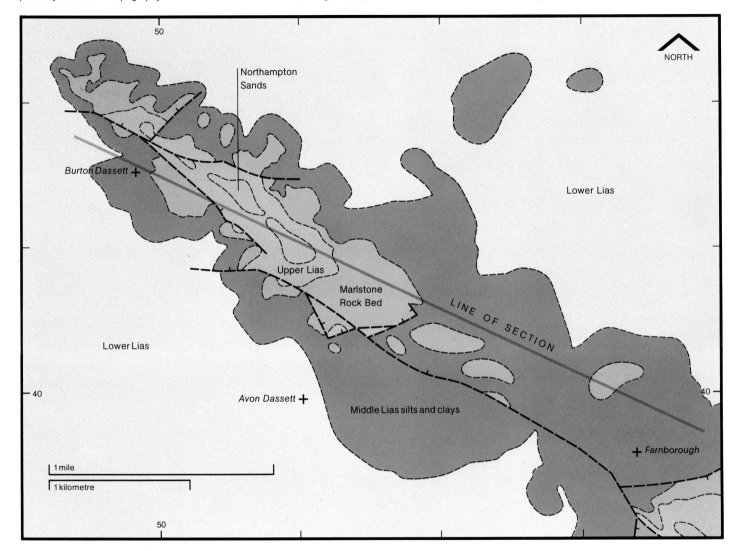

NORTH

50

Northampton
Sands

Burton Dassett +

Lower Lias

Lower Lias

Upper Lias

Marlstone
Rock Bed

LINE OF SECTION

40

40

Avon Dassett +

Middle Lias silts and clays

+ Farnborough

1 mile

1 kilometre

50

WNW

ESE

The Burton Dassett Hills of south Warwickshire might be considered a northern extremity of the Cotswolds. They form a small distinct area of typical Jurassic geology, within which the strata generally appear horizontal but show a slight regional dip to the south-east.

Around the hills lies a plain of heavy Lower Lias clay. A scatter of brash indicates the presence of a few thin bands of shelly ferruginous limestone.

As we approach the foot of the hills a spring line and slight steepening of the ground marks the base of overlying silts and clays, exposures of which yield shells of Middle Lias age. These beds are capped in a strong scarp feature by red-brown fossiliferous sandy ferruginous limestone, the Marlstone Rock Bed. Cambering presents local problems. It is commonly possible to discern a slight feature at the top of a camber, and easy to mistake it for the base of the Rock Bed—which may be shown by augering to curve downhill.

The Marlstone forms a prominent platform, from which higher slopes rise to a second and similar feature. Several old ironstone quarries reveal that the overlying strata are Upper Lias clays with up to three thin basal limestones full of ammonites. In open ground the base of these clays can be accurately located only by augering, but the occurrence of surface brash of ammonite-rich limestone is a sure sign that the Marlstone lies very near the surface. The higher scarp is of friable brown ferruginous sands barren of fossils, the Northampton Sands.

Faults within the Burton Dassett Hills are common but generally of small

16 Cambridgeshire

Hard rock bands within the chalk form surface ridges and provide persistent stratigraphic marker horizons.

Extracted from geological map sheet 205: Saffron Walden
BRG East Anglia and adjoining areas (12)

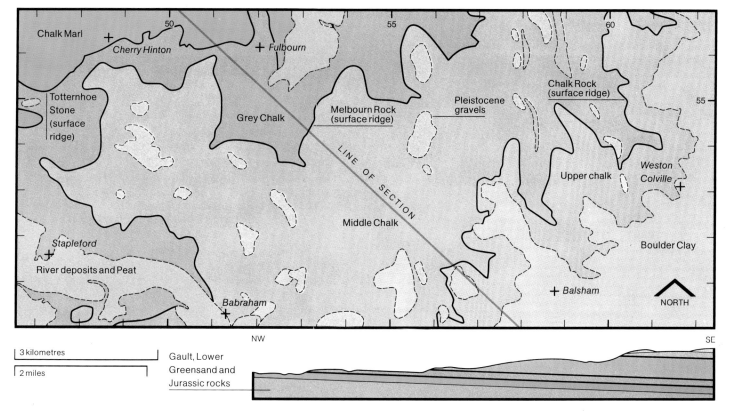

scale. Their presence is reflected in the pattern of outcrop and in localised disturbance of strata. South-east of Farnborough Northampton Sands are thrown against the Marlstone Rock Bed. The fortuitous presence of two shallow wells, one on each side of the fault, and the knowledge from mapping that the Upper Lias clays are 50 feet thick, permit the surveyor to calculate the downthrow of this fault at 65 feet to the north-north-east.

Mapping of such an area is simple and satisfying. The stratigraphical succession is perfectly reflected in the topography. Fossils abound. Geological boundaries can commonly be located precisely by used of a hand auger. Integration of the evidence is complete.

An elementary geological jigsaw, in which all the pieces are present and fall readily into place, is the chalk country. Mapping is simplified by the presence of persistent rock bands which generally give rise to distinct and traceable features. Thus the scenery is of successive small escarpments, attributed to a few tens of feet of harder strata within several hundred feet of chalk. The Totternhoe Stone lies within the Lower Chalk, above the Chalk Marl and at the base of the Grey Chalk. The overlying Middle Chalk begins with the Melbourn Rock and extends up to the Chalk Rock, which marks the base of the Upper Chalk. Typical of such gentle scarp landscapes is the country between Saffron Walden and Cambridge.

Capping the solid rocks over large areas of Britain are drift deposits, of which the most extensive is perhaps boulder clay. It is necessary to indicate the solid lines beneath this till, and our surveyor places them by calculation, estimate and

informed guess. The records of holes drilled for water and minerals are invaluable. Other prominent drifts are the old alluvial strips now represented by terrace flats above the levels of the present river flood plain. Careful mapping, followed by construction of longitudinal river profiles, enables a sequence of levels to be worked out and numbered and the history of the drainage pattern to be unravelled.

Our field geologist may soon become aware of problems requiring an alternative specialist approach. For detailed knowledge of the mineralogy and chemistry of the rocks he turns to the petrographer, for expert elucidation of the fossil evidence to the palaeontologist. Mineral veins followed across country in traces of old pits, spoil heaps and collapsed adits, all older than the oldest geological maps, may be shown by magnetic and electrical surveys to be more extensive than the surface evidence suggests. Additional work by the geophysicist throws new light on concealed structures. The geochemist, by analyses of stream waters and sediments, points to potential and unsuspected mineralised localities.

Depending on the amount and extent of superficial deposits, your map may be labelled Solid, Drift, or Solid and Drift. But on most maps all the information is there, either as broken lines showing the uncoloured solid geology beneath the drift or as pecked lines delineating uncoloured drift on solid. The symbols used are explained in the margins, and most are widely understood internationally.

From highland to lowland

If we take an armchair trip from northern Scotland to southern England, using the geological map as our guide, we will pass from the old resistant rocks and their infertile soils to younger softer strata carrying some of the richest crops in the world. And we will see how geology has exercised its influence on men from prehistoric times.

The Scottish Highlands contain great areas of high-level wet moor developed on ancient gneisses, schists, granites and quartzites. Steep-sided glens, some of them cut along faults, afforded shelter and protection to isolated communities. Movement was mainly along the valleys, and the Great Glen Fault, a wrench fault between the North-West Highlands and the Grampians, has long provided the major lowland route from coast to coast.

In the north-west, Cambrian rocks lie unconformably on Torridonian Sandstone which itself is unconformable on Lewisian Gneiss. The distinctive topographic features are west-facing scarps, mountains such as Ben More Assynt and Beinn Eighe protected by caps of Cambrian quartzite. Green fertile belts are developed on Durness Limestone.

The Moine Schists have been thrust north-westwards over these rocks, and themselves have produced a slightly less striking topography although with a number of peaks rising above 3000 feet. In the far north-east, Caithness is mainly a tableland of Old Red Sandstone flagstones, a countryside relatively flat, open and exposed. However, the flagstones have yielded friable fertile

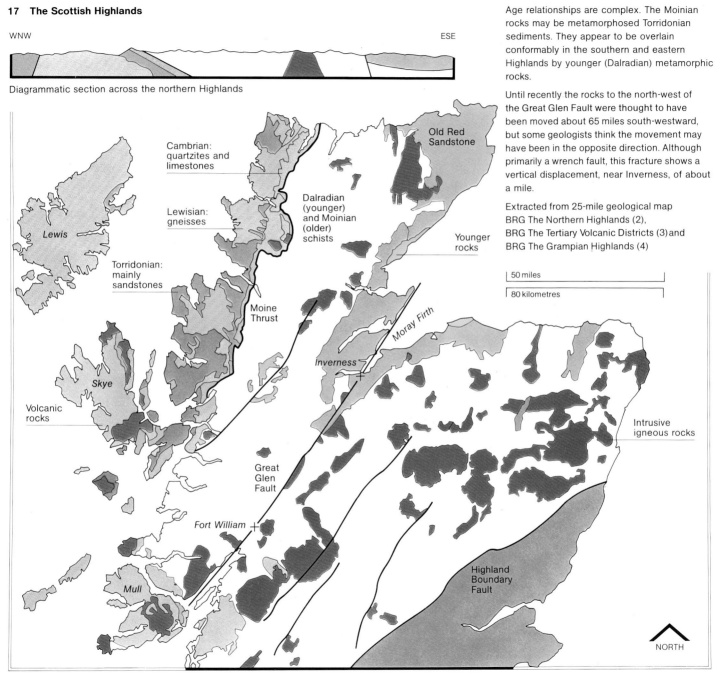

WNW   ESE

Diagrammatic section across the northern Highlands

Cambrian:
quartzites and
limestones

Lewisian:
gneisses

Lewis

Torridonian:
mainly
sandstones

Moine
Thrust

Skye

Volcanic
rocks

Great
Glen
Fault

Fort William

Mull

Dalradian
(younger)
and Moinian
(older)
schists

Old Red
Sandstone

Younger
rocks

Inverness

Moray Firth

Intrusive
igneous rocks

Highland
Boundary
Fault

NORTH

Age relationships are complex. The Moinian
rocks may be metamorphosed Torridonian
sediments. They appear to be overlain
conformably in the southern and eastern
Highlands by younger (Dalradian) metamorphic
rocks.

Until recently the rocks to the north-west of
the Great Glen Fault were thought to have
been moved about 65 miles south-westward,
but some geologists think the movement may
have been in the opposite direction. Although
primarily a wrench fault, this fracture shows a
vertical displacement, near Inverness, of about
a mile.

Extracted from 25-mile geological map
BRG The Northern Highlands (2),
BRG The Tertiary Volcanic Districts (3) and
BRG The Grampian Highlands (4)

50 miles

80 kilometres

18   The Midland Valley of Scotland

The main coals occur in the middle beds of the Carboniferous Limestone succession and in the lower part of the Coal Measures.

Oil shales are found near the base of the Carboniferous Limestone in West Lothian, Midlothian and parts of Fife.

Extracted from 25-mile geological map
BRG The Midland Valley of Scotland (5)

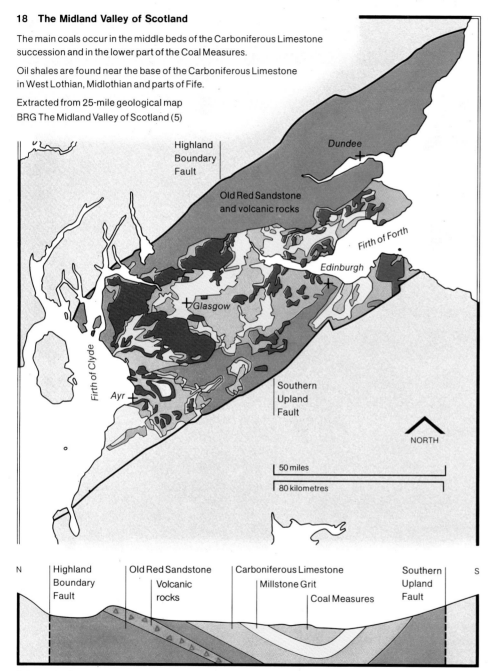

Schematic section across the Midland Valley

soils which attracted early settlement. Large plutons (intrusive bodies) of granite and gabbro are common, especially in the southern and eastern Highlands where the Moinian rocks appear to be overlain by younger (Dalradian) schists.

South of the Highlands the Midland Valley has dropped down between two great faults, the Highland Boundary Fault to the north and the Southern Upland Fault to the south, preserving Old Red Sandstone and Carboniferous rocks within a trough 50 miles wide. The direct result is a broad lowland tract of better farming and industrial development. Old Red Sandstone in the north passes eastwards beneath the rich soils of Strathmore, and is separated by the hard igneous and volcanic rocks of the Sidlaw and Ochil hills and Campsie Fells from the industrial south. Here fairly intensive farming surrounds and serves the four-fifths of the population of Scotland which has concentrated around the coal-bearing rocks and oil-shales and their attendant heavy industry. Within this central undulating plain, mainly of Carboniferous strata, many sharp irregularities are due to the presence of igneous rocks. Examples are the dolerite hills of Fife, the Castle Rock of Stirling and the volcanics of the Bathgate Hills and Arthur's Seat.

In the Southern Uplands and the border country of the Cheviots, Lower Palaeozoic sediments with granites and volcanic rocks have fathered high moorland whose sheep support the local woollen industry. In the lower reaches of the valleys boulder clay soils permit mixed farming, as they do over much of northern England, but little agricultural improvement is possible on the high ground and Kielder Water lies within the largest man-made forest in Europe.

19 Wigtown and Kirkcudbrightshire

Granite intrusions and metamorphism in the western part of the Southern Uplands have produced scenery reminiscent of the Highlands.

Extracted from 25-mile geological map
BRG The South of Scotland (6)

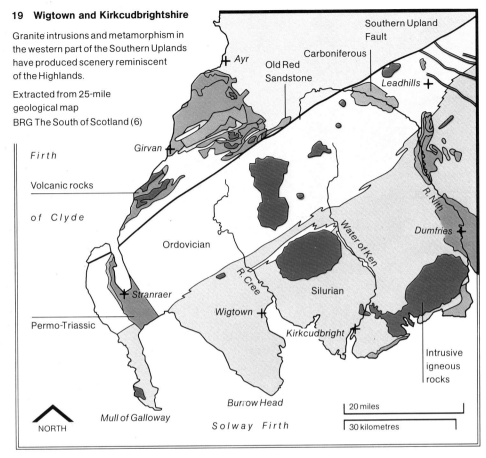

20 Hadrian's Wall and the Whin Sill

Crags of igneous rock were utilised to advantage as a foundation for this great frontier fortification of the Roman Empire.

Extracted from 1:253 400 geological map sheets 3 & 4 Carlisle, Keswick and part of the Isle of Man, and Newcastle upon Tyne, Stockton, etc.
BRG Northern England (7)

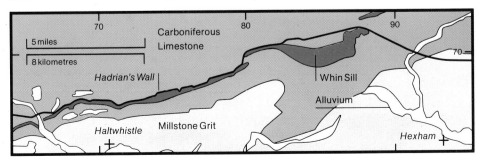

In general the rocks lie in bands running from north-east to south-west, with the oldest rocks in the north-west and the youngest in the south-east. Wigtownshire and Kirkcudbrightshire possess some scenery of semi-Highland aspect, of ridges, corries and hill-lochs, due in part to the presence of granitic intrusions and metamorphism of adjacent sediments.

Coal mining in north-east England created a region overdependent on mining, heavy engineering, shipbuilding and steel. The westward extension of the outcrop of the Coal Measures and Millstone Grit, in which thick gritstones are less common than they are farther south, marks the Tyne Gap, one of the rare east–west corridors across northern England. Immediately north of this gap runs the Whin Sill, a striking feature of intrusive dolerite utilised by the Romans to increase the strategic importance of Hadrian's Wall.

To the south the northern Pennines and the Lake District lie on either side of the Permo-Triassic rocks of the Eden Valley. Both these upland areas have been worked for lead and slate. The Lake District owes its character as a compact unit of semi-Alpine scenery and a National Park to a combination of rock type and glacial history. The rugged volcanic rocks of Borrowdale rise to Scafell Pike, the highest peak in England.

The strata of the Pennines are tilted eastwards and faulted along their western edge. Carboniferous Limestone in the north and in the Peak District carries lead which once supported a mining industry. Now fluorspar is worked, with lead as a byproduct, and the limestone is quarried for a variety of industrial uses. Between the two limestone areas the high ground is formed of Millstone Grit with a patchy peat cover. Sheep-rearing remains the major land use of the

21 The Lake District

Slates, volcanic rocks and glaciation have produced scenery of somewhat Alpine aspect.

Extracted from 10-mile geological map, north and south sheets
BRG Northern England (7)

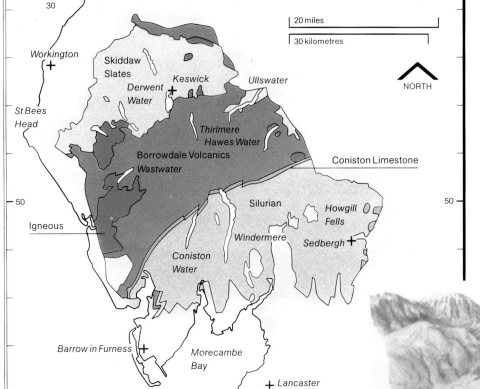

Diagrammatic section

fells and dales, but to either side of the Pennines lie industrial areas such as have ever grown around coal mines.

North Wales shows an imperfect but broad correlation between topography and rock-type. The mountains of Snowdonia coincide with a downfold of Ordovician rocks between the older strata of Llanberis to the north-west and the Harlech Dome to the south. They contain much hard volcanic rock, which has proved resistant to erosion, and mountains of similar Ordovician ashes and lavas – the Moelwyns, the Arenigs, the Arans and Cader Idris – skirt the Harlech Dome. The dome itself is rough country of Cambrian grits, shales and flaggy sandstones with dioritic intrusions. Slates of North Wales have been won from enormous quarries and mines, and some of the latter are now proving a popular tourist attraction. Disseminated copper has been explored at Coed y Brennin.

22 Sedbergh

A contrast in landscape between Carboniferous country in the foreground and the Silurian rocks of the Lake District Howgill Fells beyond.

BRG The Pennines and adjacent areas (8)

23 Northern England

The geological map of northern England shows high ground of pre-Carboniferous rocks, the Lake District, surrounded by younger rocks and separated from the Pennines by red sandstones and shales in the Vale of Eden. Successively younger rocks crop out eastwards from the Pennines.

A three-dimensional view shows that the region is flanked by coalfield basins, and that the old rocks of the Lake District have been uplifted in the core of a great dome.

The presence of the Weardale Granite was suggested by gravity measurements and proved by a borehole at Rookhope.

BRG Northern England (7)
BRG The Pennines and adjacent areas (8)

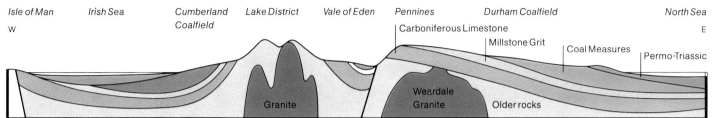

24 North Wales

A region of hard rocks and rugged scenery.

Extracted from 10-mile geological sheet, south sheet
BRG North Wales (18)

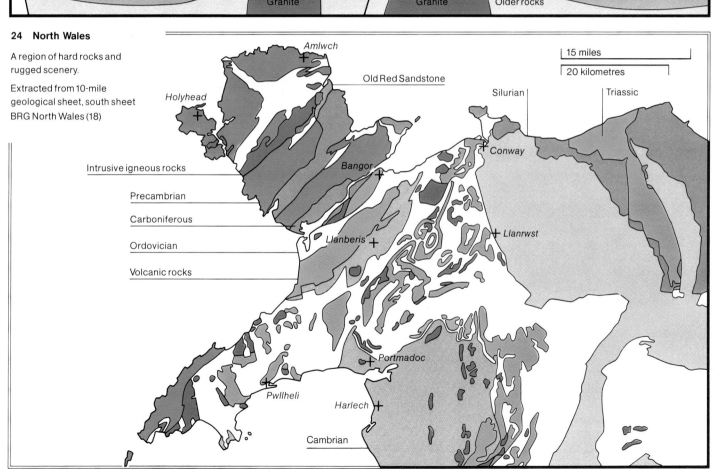

To the east and south lies generally undulating country formed by softer Upper Ordovician and Silurian sediments. Carboniferous rocks of Flintshire and Denbighshire dip generally eastwards, giving dip-and-scarp scenery where not concealed by drift deposits; the heathy Denbighshire Moors have developed on Silurian shales and grits.

The Ordovician and Silurian grits and shales east and south of Aberystwyth have formed bleak infertile moorland. Igneous rocks have introduced more rugged and craggy scenery near Builth and round the south-west coastline between Fishguard and St Bride's Bay.

Richer soils developed on the gently dipping Old Red Sandstone north of the South Wales coalfield support more arable and dairy farming. They mantle relatively low-lying ground, interrupted by the heights of Mynydd Epynt, the Black Mountains and the Brecon Beacons. The major scarp of the Brecon Beacons, formed by grits and conglomerates of the Upper Old Red Sandstone, is succeeded to the south by parallel ridges of Millstone Grit and Pennant Sandstone. Within the coalfield the Coal Measures are gashed by narrow mining valleys, and beyond the low country of the Vale of Glamorgan lie the minor hills of the Gower peninsula.

To the east, in the Welsh Borders south of the Shropshire plain, the Upper Silurian rocks of the Long Mountain give way south-eastwards to the Ordovician Shelve area and its jagged ridge of quartzite, the Stiperstones. The Long Mynd consists of hard Precambrian sediments and is flanked by ancient volcanic rocks well exposed in the Caradoc Hills. Farther south-east is the Ordovician and Silurian scarp and dale country of Hoar Edge and Wenlock Edge, and a plateau of Old Red Sandstone

25 South Wales

Scarps of the northern flank of the South Wales coalfield
BRG South Wales (19)

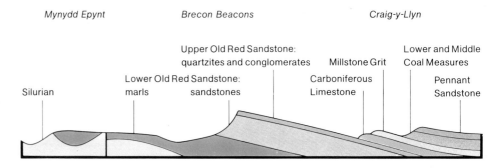

26 The Gower Peninsula

Hills and valleys reflect the underlying geological structure
BRG South Wales (19)

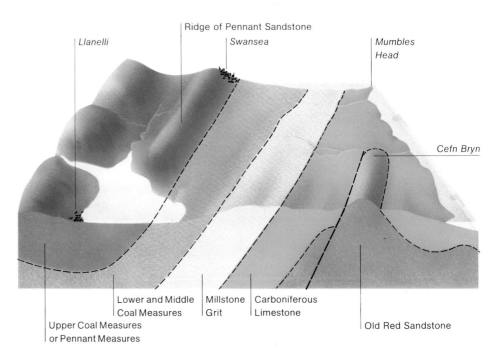

27 The Welsh Marches

Ridges of hard ancient rock give way south-eastwards to the scarps and dales between Much Wenlock and Craven Arms and the rolling Old Red Sandstone landscape of Hereford

Extracted from 10-mile geological map, south sheet
BRG The Welsh Borderland (11)

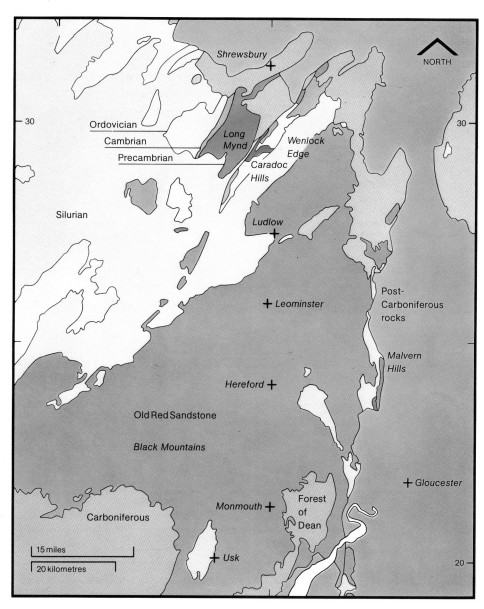

upon which Brown Clee and Titterstone Clee sit as outliers of Carboniferous rock protected from erosion by dolerite. Extensive rolling countryside of Old Red Sandstone stretches south towards Monmouth, the older rocks of the Malverns and Usk and the Carboniferous of the Forest of Dean.

South of the Bristol Channel lies the south-west peninsula of England. Here a mining boom of the 19th century, based on metalliferous ores injected into Devonian and Carboniferous rocks from the same source whence came the great Cornubian granites, was followed by decline and depression only partially relieved by increased exploitation of china clay, an alteration product of granite, and Palaeogene ball clay. Despite a small mining revival, it is the tourist appeal of the moorlands and the coast, equally the products of geological history, which promises most to the prosperity of the region.

Midland counties of England, in part good, well-timbered farmland on Triassic and Jurassic rocks and glacial clays and gravels, in part populous and drab near the coalfields of Warwickshire and Leicestershire, are traversed by the scarp of the Oolites, which runs from the Dorset coast to the Cleveland Hills and forms a geological and topographic boundary between the old 'hard' north and west, of highland and heavy industry, and the young 'soft' south and east of rolling downland and fen. When lowland England was densely forested such 'high-ways' were the long-distance footpaths of Neolithic Man. He could walk this Jurassic Way for 300 miles. A diversion from its northern end took him along the chalk ridge of south-east Yorkshire and Lincolnshire to The Wash, and its southern stretch passed close to Salisbury Plain whence tracks followed the chalk scarps of the Chilterns and the North Downs to East Anglia and Folkestone.

Some of the northernmost Jurassic rocks in England contain the Cleveland Ironstone which fed the furnaces of Tees-side. Farther south low-grade Jurassic iron ores of Lincolnshire, Leicestershire, Rutland, Northampton-shire and Oxfordshire have been quarried over thousands of acres and the land generally well restored.

Drift-covered chalk and Pliocene and Pleistocene sands and clays of south Lincolnshire, Norfolk and Suffolk have supported rich pastures and arable crops, but some areas of heathland around Thetford are forested. The Broads themselves originated as peat cuttings in the Middle Ages.

Within the Chalk uplands which surround the London basin there lie the remains of a much degraded smaller parallel scarp of Tertiary sands. The centre of the basin is underlain by sticky London Clay, the topmost beds of which are locally sandy. Bagshot Sands

28 The Cornubian Granite

The exposed granites of south-west England are cupolas on the roof of a single batholith. That of Haig Fras is an underwater outcrop.

BRG South-West England (17)

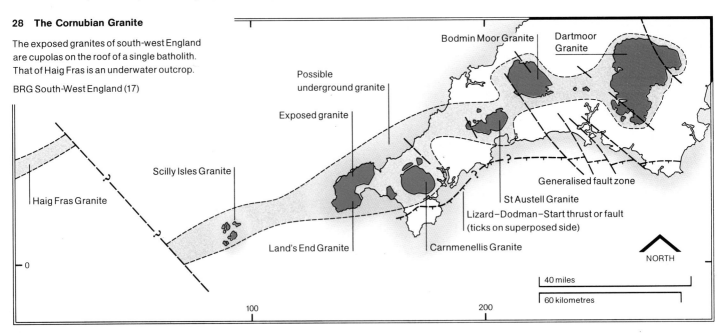

29 The Welsh Borders to the Chilterns

The resistant rocks of the Oolites form a ridge running from Dorset to Yorkshire that separates the industrial north and west from the younger rocks of the south and east.

BRG The Welsh Borderland (11)
BRG London and the Thames Valley (13)
BRG Bristol and Gloucester District (16)

30 Trackways

The long-distance footpaths of early man evolved along ridges, especially those of the Jurassic Oolites and the Chalk.

These ridgeways were probably dry and free of forest and were grazed by stock of the earliest pastoralists. In contrast the lower ground was wet and densely wooded.

Extracted from 25-mile geological map

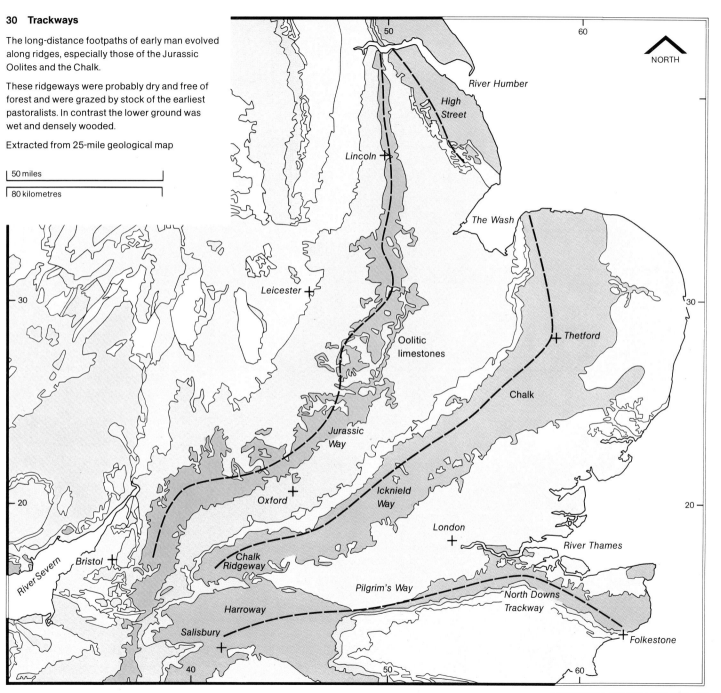

A major syncline and anticline beneath the Home Counties

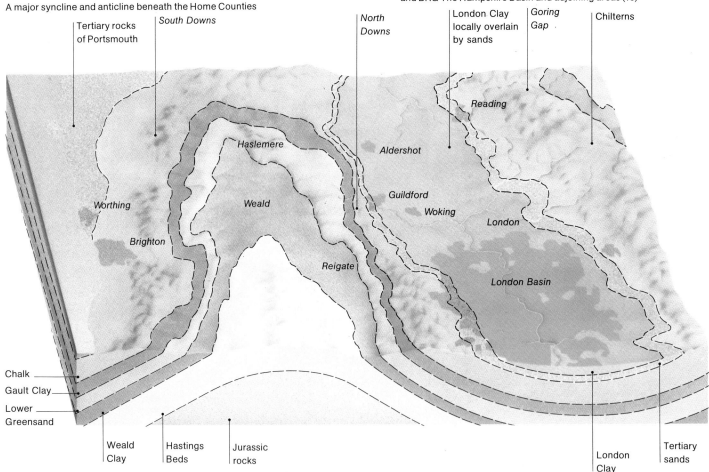

Tertiary rocks of Portsmouth

South Downs

North Downs

London Clay locally overlain by sands

Goring Gap

Chilterns

Haslemere

Aldershot

Reading

Worthing

Weald

Guildford

Woking

London

Brighton

Reigate

London Basin

Chalk

Gault Clay

Lower Greensand

Weald Clay

Hastings Beds

Jurassic rocks

London Clay

Tertiary sands

mantle the clays in places, and especially in the area Woking–Chertsey–Aldershot–Wokingham, giving rise to heathland which makes a pleasing contrast with the featureless clay country. Lighter soils occur also over patches of Pleistocene gravel.

To the south, in the anticline of the Weald, the Chalk Downs encircle a narrow low-lying belt of Gault clay which itself rings the Lower Greensand escarpment. These sandy beds rise to a height of almost 1000 feet at Leith Hill; they are well developed on the northern and western flanks of the anticline, and contain cherts and limestones, but in the south they are softer and thinner. Within this scarp is a broad band of low heavy clay land overlying the soft Weald Clay, and the centre of the Weald is a deeply dissected area of Hastings Beds sands and clays rising locally to over 700 feet. The iron industry of Sussex and Kent used ores from Wealden strata.

Our tour started in an area whose development has taken place largely within limits set by Nature, and we end it in an area where an expanding modern commercial society is imposing its will on the countryside. The contrasts are rarely so sharp, but your geological map will point to the gains and losses beneath the soil wherever we exercise a choice between one use of land and another.

Maps and minerals

The distribution of minerals, and hence the pattern of exploitation, is reflected on the geological map. Treatment plant, smelters and refineries may be placed at sites convenient for transport, power or labour, but the raw materials are extracted from where the geologist has found them. Britain is still well endowed, but as profitable deposits have declined into worked-out areas the boom of the past has too often become the development problem of the present. Major difficulties in old coal, iron and salt fields, and in Cornish mining areas, are repeated on a reduced scale elsewhere, as around the lead mines of the Pennine dales.

Lodes and placers

Metallic minerals may be concentrated by magmatic processes and injected into the surrounding rocks to form veins or lodes. These are shown on the geological map with an indication of their content. High-temperature minerals, say those of tin and wolfram, are deposited close to the parent melt, lower temperature minerals, perhaps with arsenic and copper, travel a greater distance, and farther still may be found nickel, uranium, lead, zinc and iron.

Weathering and erosion of lodes and veins at surface can produce concentration as the heavy grains collect on river or stream bed, and any area of upland metalliferous mineralisation is likely to contain such placer deposits in the alluvium of its valleys.

Evaporites

Substances such as gypsum, celestine, potash and rock salt, present as layers interbedded with other strata, have formed by evaporation of solutions, and although by their nature they produce little direct surface effect, underground solution can lead to subsidence and the appearance of pools or meres called flashes. This is quite common in Cheshire.

Sedimentary ironstone

Sedimentary iron ores occur in Mesozoic rocks from Yorkshire to Dorset and commonly appear on the map as distinct formations of ferruginous limestone or sandstone. In the field they appear as prominent scarps, hill caps

32 Anglesey

Igneous activity which injected the felsite intrusion of Parys Mountain into Palaeozoic sediments also introduced associated copper sulphides.

Copper ores were discovered in 1768. Amlwch, which in 1766 consisted of six fishermen's houses, had grown by 1801 to a town of 6000 people of whom 1500 worked in the copper mines. About 10 years of peak output were followed by slow decline, and mining ended during the 1870s. The population of Amlwch is now about 3000.

This is a perfect illustration in miniature of the many mining booms which have lit the world industrial stage.

Extracted from geological map: Anglesey special sheet
BRG North Wales (18)

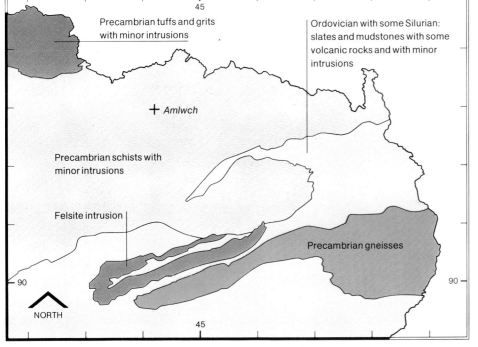

Precambrian tuffs and grits with minor intrusions

Ordovician with some Silurian: slates and mudstones with some volcanic rocks and with minor intrusions

+ Amlwch

Precambrian schists with minor intrusions

Felsite intrusion

Precambrian gneisses

NORTH

2 miles

3 kilometres

and plateaus among soft clays and silts and their lines of outcrop are additionally marked by red soils, brash and an abundance of small pits. They represent some of the easiest of all geological formations to follow across country. The Cleveland ore gave rise to steelworks at Middlesborough, the Northampton Sand at Corby and the Frodingham Ironstone at Scunthorpe.

33   The Frodingham Ironstone Field

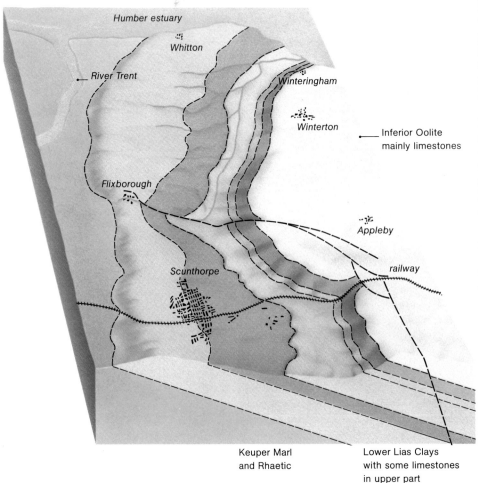

are sand and gravel, limestone and clay. All are worked at surface and all are shown on the geological map. Sand and gravel cost so much to transport that sources near to building operations are considered essential. Extensive flooded gravel workings in the Thames valley attest the demand around London.

Limestone, which feeds the chemical, steel, glass and cement industries and agriculture, is similarly widespread both geologically and geographically, and it is rare to locate a limestone on the ground from its representation on the map without discovering numerous traces of pitting and quarrying. The Carboniferous Limestone gives us more than two-thirds of our supplies, but much chalk is quarried in the south and east of England.

The Oxford Clay runs from Dorset to Lincolnshire and is our most important source of brick clay. In this industry, in contrast to sand and gravel, it has been found possible to work on such a large scale that transport costs are acceptable. Hence the enormous pits and brickworks of Peterborough and Bedford.

Limestones within the Lower Lias clays are responsible for the small scarp west of Scunthorpe.

The Middle Lias is largely of silts and clays but an impersistent cap of ferruginous calcareous sandstone, the Marlstone Rock Bed, produces a small feature.

BRG Eastern England from the Tees to The Wash (9)

Upper Lias Clays
Middle Lias
Lower Lias Clays
Frodingham Ironstone

Other bulk minerals

Coal has probably had a greater effect on the evolution of our country than any other of our natural resources. Swampy forest debris has been preserved as compressed layers interbedded with other sediments, and isolated in basins on which have developed our coalfields.

Our other principal bulk minerals

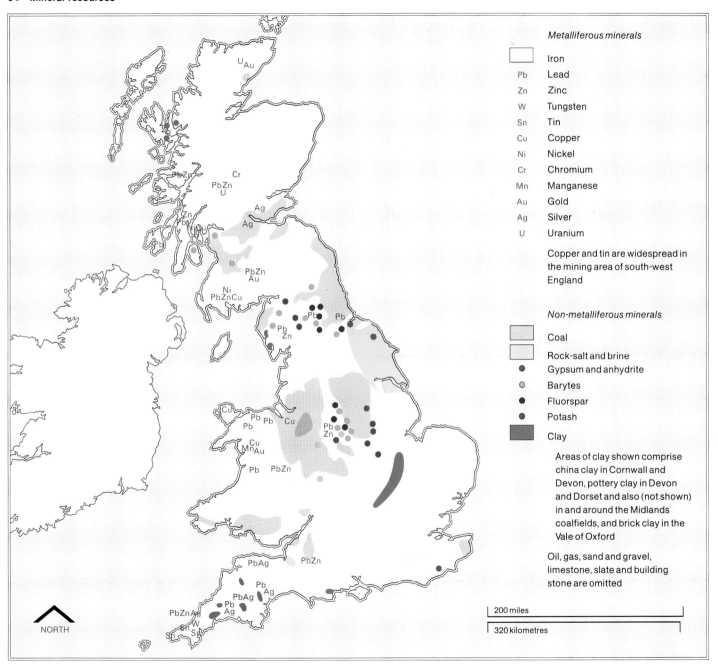

Metalliferous minerals

	Iron
Pb	Lead
Zn	Zinc
W	Tungsten
Sn	Tin
Cu	Copper
Ni	Nickel
Cr	Chromium
Mn	Manganese
Au	Gold
Ag	Silver
U	Uranium

Copper and tin are widespread in the mining area of south-west England

Non-metalliferous minerals

	Coal
	Rock-salt and brine
●	Gypsum and anhydrite
○	Barytes
●	Fluorspar
●	Potash
	Clay

Areas of clay shown comprise china clay in Cornwall and Devon, pottery clay in Devon and Dorset and also (not shown) in and around the Midlands coalfields, and brick clay in the Vale of Oxford

Oil, gas, sand and gravel, limestone, slate and building stone are omitted

200 miles

320 kilometres

NORTH

Mapping the industrial wastelands

All the counties in which mining has been conducted possess a legacy of dereliction, but as sand and gravel take over from coal as our biggest extractive industry the geographical balance may change. Increased attention is being given to the restoring of ground disfigured by spoil heaps and open pits, both as a means of reclaiming land for use and to avoid the dangers inherent in such derelict landscapes. Knowledge of the nature of the spoil and of the geology beneath the tip enables stability to be assessed, not least by an appraisal of possible build-up of water in the waste or trapped under it.

Holes left by industry make useful receptables for refuse, but whether such disposal is safe depends on the local geology. Waste disposal on permeable strata requires a detailed knowledge of the surrounding rocks and the movement and utilisation of groundwater. A disused slate quarry, on the other hand, may be completely safe.

35 Waste disposal

The geological map will show where the gradual extension of a waste tip across a spring may lead to build up of water in the spoil and a subsequent dangerous mud flow, triggered by abnormally heavy rain or perhaps a slight earth tremor.

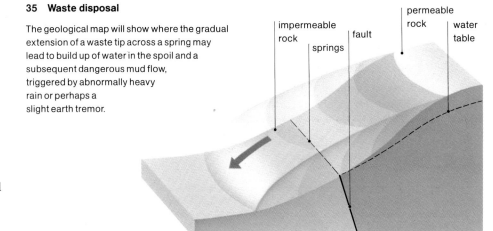

impermeable rock | springs | fault | permeable rock | water table

Drainage from refuse tipped in this old chalk pit would pass rapidly into groundwater along fissures characteristic of limestone country.

Leachate from refuse in an old gravel pit will travel quickly through the intergranular spaces of the gravel, perhaps to pollute nearby wells.

river terrace gravel

well

bedrock

alluvium

Mineral search

The search on land

The modern prospector uses a range of techniques not available to the old miner. A magnetometer survey may locate concealed iron ores, and through an association of iron and mixed sulphides can also lead to the detection of non-ferrous metal. Electromagnetic surveys have been useful in tracing sulphide ore bodies. Seismic investigations are most important in looking for oil and gas. Transmission of shock waves and recording their return indicates depths to reflecting and refracting surfaces and possibly, from a knowledge of wave speeds in known rocks, the nature of the geological formations. Other approaches include the measurement of natural radioactivity, and most methods have been adapted for use in the logging of boreholes. Gravimeters measure the density of the underlying rock and permit theoretical calculations about the nature and depth of bodies responsible for gravity 'highs' and 'lows'. These geophysical techniques, although mainly used in mineral search, are also applicable to geological mapping.

Geochemical field investigations revolve around the collection and analysis for specific elements of stream sediments, soils, water, rocks and even plants. Plotting the results for individual elements or particular combinations of elements, followed by comparison with the geological map, can both afford a check of geological boundaries and trace economic minerals back to their parent ore body.

The search at sea

Mineral search is increasingly concerned with undersea exploration, and this has led to attempts to map the continental shelf by means of divers, manned and unmanned submersibles, drilling, bottom sampling and many of the instrumental techniques pioneered on land. It is likely that more and more coastal maps will show submarine geology, although the detail will rarely match that of inland areas.

Britain dredges around 10 million tons a year of submarine sand and gravel, but the really dramatic offshore developments of recent years have centred round oil and gas. Exploitation at present confined to continental shelf depths of a few hundreds of feet will inevitably be extended to the deep sea floor.

36 Geophysical surveys around northern Dartmoor

BRG South-West England (17)

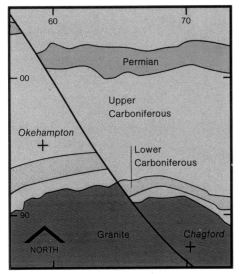

Geology

10 miles

10 kilometres

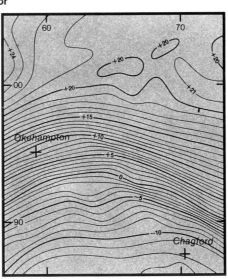

Gravity anomalies (contoured in milligals). The negative gravity anomaly is caused by the granite being of lower density than the surrounding rocks.

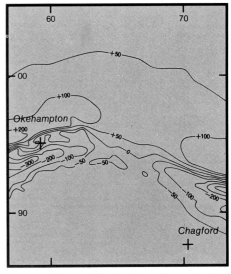

Aeromagnetic anomalies (contoured in nanoteslas). Magnetic disturbances skirting the granite are probably due to mineralisation in the Lower Carboniferous rocks and to basic intrusions.

Water supplies

The water we drink is taken either from streams and rivers or from underground reserves accumulated in permeable strata such as sandstone or limestone. Both sources are governed by geology, both may be understood, explained and predicted by reference to the geological map.

Most of Britain has a moderate rainfall and water resources to meet existing needs; the problems are not of availability but of methods of exploitation. Surface supplies predominate in the wet western areas of old hard rocks, groundwater is tapped extensively in the Midlands and the south.

The Triassic sandstones and pebble beds constitute important aquifers and may be seen from maps of solid geology to crop out from Stockton-on-Tees to Nottingham and extensively in Staffordshire, northern Shropshire, Cheshire, Lancashire and the Vale of Eden. Further reference to the maps will reveal where the various Triassic sandstones pass beneath younger strata and may therefore be tapped at depth by boreholes. Especially important in trapping water within these rocks is the widespread Keuper Marl of the Midlands, an impermeable seal whose presence commonly creates artesian conditions. However, the Chalk is the most important aquifer in Britain.

London's public supplies are drawn mainly from the Thames. The rest of south-east England is supplied in part by surface abstraction from rivers but mostly by groundwater from the Chalk.

37 Water supply

Artesian water is obtained when an aquifer sandwiched between impermeable strata is tapped by a well situated below the level of the water table.

Groundwater may be impounded naturally in much the same way as a surface reservoir is dammed – perhaps by impermeable strata or unfractured igneous intrusions.

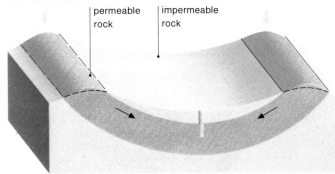

permeable rock   impermeable rock

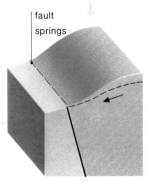

fault springs

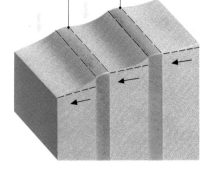

springs   springs   springs

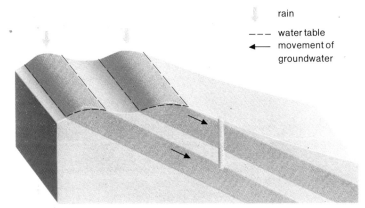

rain
- - - water table
← movement of groundwater

An impermeable stratum may produce a perched water table above the general level of saturation within permeable rocks.

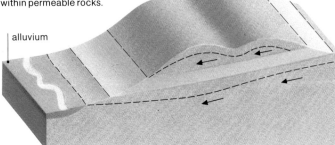

alluvium

An understanding of the map will lead to recognition of the basin-like structure of the lower Thames valley, and how the chalk aquifer may be tapped by drilling through the London Clay.

The vital contrast between sandy aquifers, including the important Triassic sandstones, and limestone aquifers such as the Chalk or the Carboniferous Limestone, is that in sandy aquifers the water moves steadily through the spaces between the grains but in limestone aquifers solution of the rock itself creates fissure systems through which water may migrate very quickly.

When surface water is to be impounded in reservoirs geological maps of the reservoir area give some indication of the likely underground leakage. They are vital in the neighbourhood of the dam itself, in guiding the engineer in his search for a firm foundation, in influencing the type and design of the dam and in governing the measures necessary to create as watertight a seal as possible.

Water entering limestone creates solution channels along joints and bedding planes, and groundwater moves through these fissures.

Strength and stability

The engineer turning from water resources to any other major project is likely to find his need for geological maps undiminished. Whether he is siting a big office block, a bridge, or a nuclear power station, constructing a runway or a motorway, excavating a cutting or driving a tunnel, he must know the rocks he is dealing with. How strong are they, and what loads will they bear? Are they watertight or will groundwater present problems? Can material dug from one place make a satisfactory embankment at another, and, if not, does the geological map point to a nearby source? This is territory where geologist, engineer, geophysicist and soil mechanics expert converge, and distinctions become blurred.

An earth dam can be built on a variety of foundations but the cut-off wall, of clay or concrete, must be carried down into impermeable rock or to a depth which reduces leakage to an acceptable amount. The load is widely spread. In contrast, a concrete dam is much narrower and requires to be securely keyed in to

Special maps may be drawn for special purposes, perhaps hydrogeological or engineering. Information about the nature of the solid rocks, drifts and soils – grain sizes, textures, thicknesses, fractures, weathering, alteration, strengths, permeabilities – then takes precedence over such aspects of 'pure' geology as classification of formations, age and fossil content. Evidence of pitting and mining is commonly important for such geotechnical maps. Peat bogs, marshes, made ground and signs of subsidence are shown, as are the permanence or otherwise of streams and their response to heavy rain. Seepages, swallow holes, caves, boreholes and wells are recorded, together with the nature of slopes, scarps and cliffs and evidence of slips and solifluction.

Separate maps might be necessary for surface drainage, groundwater, soils, drift deposits, bedrock, tectonic structures and superficial structures. But the foundation of all will be a three-dimensional view of the underlying rocks, the geological map.

suitably competent rocks in the valley floor and sides. Foundation rocks may dictate a composite structure. Thus the dam at Cow Green, in upper Teesdale, is of concrete where founded on the Whin Sill dolerite and of earth where founded on boulder clay.

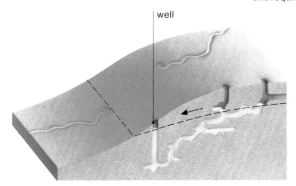

well

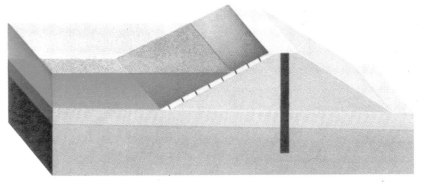

Plans and planners

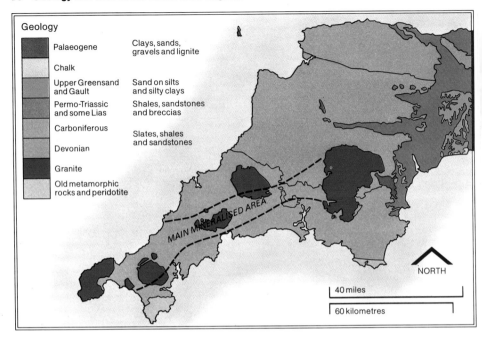

Geology

- Palaeogene — Clays, sands, gravels and lignite
- Chalk
- Upper Greensand and Gault — Sand on silts and silty clays
- Permo-Triassic and some Lias — Shales, sandstones and breccias
- Carboniferous
- Devonian — Slates, shales and sandstones
- Granite
- Old metamorphic rocks and peridotite

MAIN MINERALISED AREA

NORTH

40 miles

60 kilometres

Mounting pressures on the land in recent years have highlighted the variety of fields in which good geological maps are fundamental to any comprehensive planning of land use. It is important to know not only if a development is geologically feasible, but also whether the geology itself suggests alternatives or offers any future potential in terms of natural resources.

Mining and quarrying are emotive subjects, particularly as many mineralised areas lie within landscapes of outstanding beauty. But whatever we feel about the economic and aesthetic costs and benefits of exploitation, there cannot be an informed decision without a knowledge of what is there. A detailed geological map guides the making of an assessment, the politician weighs the larger issues.

Probably our most important natural resource is the land itself, and by far the most active consumer of that resource is urban spread. Almost every other programme of land use is reversible—farming, forestry, military training, recreation, water supply. Even the wastelands created by the major extraction industries are capable of repair, at least on the scale of working so far practised in this country.

Clearly, then, we must wherever possible avoid building over valuable reserves of sand and gravel, clay, limestone, indeed of any minerals which would be permanently lost by the development. The place to look for a summary of the situation is the geological map. We must also try not to divert our new town to an area of high amenity

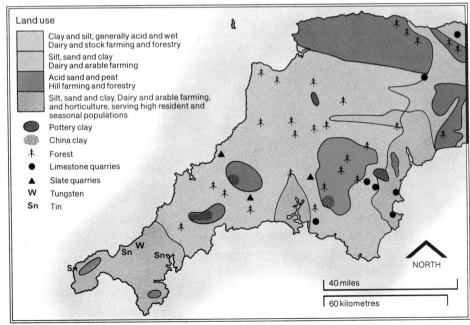

Land use

- Clay and silt, generally acid and wet. Dairy and stock farming and forestry
- Silt, sand and clay. Dairy and arable farming
- Acid sand and peat. Hill farming and forestry
- Silt, sand and clay. Dairy and arable farming, and horticulture, serving high resident and seasonal populations
- Pottery clay
- China clay
- Forest
- Limestone quarries
- Slate quarries
- W Tungsten
- Sn Tin

NORTH

40 miles

60 kilometres

value or on to rich farmland—both the products of their local geology. So we are left with poor land of little scenic value, areas which may be given up with least loss, if loss there must be; and it is fitting to conclude with the realisation that even where the geologist has failed to locate mineral wealth, where his rocks have yielded neither great landscape nor rich soil, nevertheless his maps offer the foundation to a solution of one of the major problems of modern times.

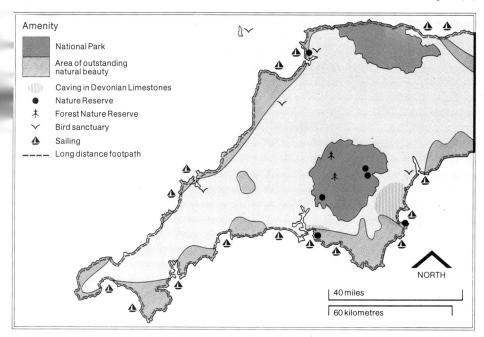

Amenity

- National Park
- Area of outstanding natural beauty
- Caving in Devonian Limestones
- ● Nature Reserve
- ⚘ Forest Nature Reserve
- ⌄ Bird sanctuary
- ⚓ Sailing
- ---- Long distance footpath

NORTH

40 miles
60 kilometres

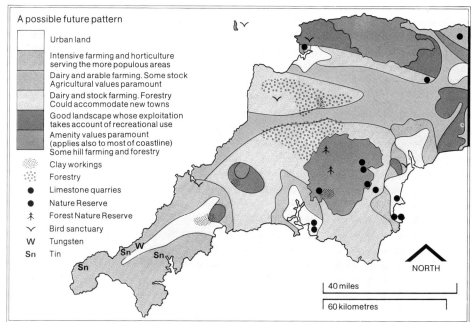

A possible future pattern

- Urban land
- Intensive farming and horticulture serving the more populous areas
- Dairy and arable farming. Some stock Agricultural values paramount
- Dairy and stock farming. Forestry Could accommodate new towns
- Good landscape whose exploitation takes account of recreational use
- Amenity values paramount (applies also to most of coastline) Some hill farming and forestry
- Clay workings
- Forestry
- ● Limestone quarries
- ● Nature Reserve
- ⚘ Forest Nature Reserve
- ⌄ Bird sanctuary
- W Tungsten
- Sn Tin

NORTH

40 miles
60 kilometres

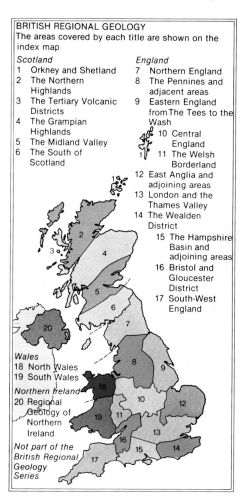

BRITISH REGIONAL GEOLOGY
The areas covered by each title are shown on the index map

Scotland
1 Orkney and Shetland
2 The Northern Highlands
3 The Tertiary Volcanic Districts
4 The Grampian Highlands
5 The Midland Valley
6 The South of Scotland

England
7 Northern England
8 The Pennines and adjacent areas
9 Eastern England from The Tees to the Wash
10 Central England
11 The Welsh Borderland
12 East Anglia and adjoining areas
13 London and the Thames Valley
14 The Wealden District
15 The Hampshire Basin and adjoining areas
16 Bristol and Gloucester District
17 South-West England

Wales
18 North Wales
19 South Wales

Northern Ireland
20 Regional Geology of Northern Ireland

Not part of the British Regional Geology Series

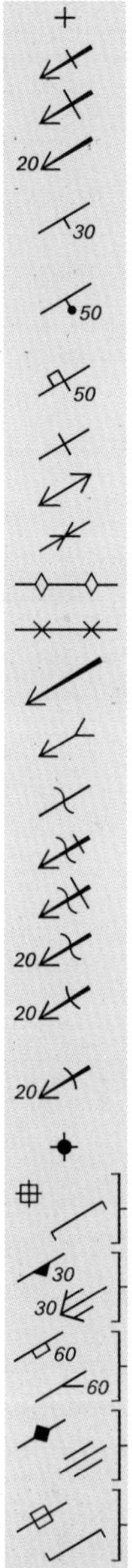

Geological maps

+	Horizontal strata
	Gently inclined strata
	Highly inclined strata
20	Inclined strata, dip in degrees
30	Inclined strata, dip in degrees, normal succession
50	Inclined strata, dip in degrees, direction of succession unknown
50	Inclined strata, dip in degrees, inverted succession
	Vertical strata
	Anticline
	Syncline
	Anticlinal axis
	Synclinal axis
	Regional dip of strata
	Direction in which younger beds come on
	Minor fold, axis horizontal
	Minor fold with gentle plunge
	Minor fold with steep plunge
20	Minor fold, plunge in degrees
20	Major or intermediate anticline, plunge in degrees
20	Major or intermediate syncline, plunge in degrees
	Horizontal cleavage
	Horizontal joints
30 / 30	Cleavage, inclined, dip in degrees
60 / 60	Inclined joints, dip in degrees
	Vertical cleavage
	Vertical joints

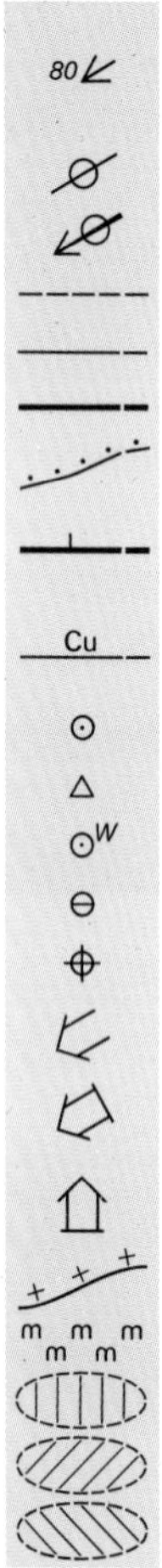

80	Inclination of dyke, sheet, igneous contact, vein or fault plane, angle in degrees
	Glacial striae
	Glacial striae with direction of ice flow
-----	Geological boundary, drift
———	Geological boundary, solid
▬▬▬	Coal crop
	Base of lava flow, dots above base
▬▬	Fault, crossmark indicates downthrow side
Cu	Mineral vein with chemical symbol of significant element
⊙	Borehole
△	Borehole, exact site uncertain
⊙W	Water well or borehole
⊖	Shaft
⊕	Abandoned shaft
	Adit, showing direction of entry
	Abandoned adit, showing direction of entry
	Abandoned adit, direction of entry unknown
+ + +	Outer margin of metamorphic aureole
m m m / m m	Metamorphic aureole
	Landslip
	Worked out opencast mineral area
	Made ground

The main omissions from this list are symbols modified from those for normal bedded strata to apply to other planar structures (such as corrugated strata, axial planes of folds and foliation) and to indicate underground observations.

There are also special symbols for the attitude of lineation, for various sorts of fossil bands and for additional glacial features.

Geological maps of the United Kingdom, where good topographic maps exist and there are few problems of access, are based on direct observation by the field geologist supplemented by records of construction sites, boreholes, mining explorations, and instrumental surveys. The factual data are fashioned into a coherent scheme by interpretation of land form.

Survey since about 1845 has been generally at a scale of 1:10 560 or 1:10 000; of the United Kingdom's land surface area of 245 000 square kilometres, about four fifths has now been geologically surveyed at this scale.

Publication is generally at 1:50 000, in a series which covers the United Kingdom in about 560 sheets. Depending on the extent of the superficial deposits, each sheet is issued either in separate solid and drift editions or in a combined edition. Maps at other scales are also published: a full list appears opposite.

Most of the maps are published for the Institute by the Ordnance Survey and are available from Ordnance Survey Agents. The maps are also obtainable from the Bookshop, Geological Museum, Exhibition Road, London SW7 2DE, and from the Institute's offices at Ring Road Halton, Leeds LS15 8TQ, and Murchison House, West Mains Road, Edinburgh EH9 3LA. Northern Ireland maps are obtainable from the Geological Survey of Northern Ireland, 20 College Gardens, Belfast BT9 6BS.

Printed in the UK for HMSO   Dd 496313   9.83